# DENARIUS

## A NEW WORLD CURRENCY

2017-2018
A CONCISE DENARIUS HISTORY BOOK

**Denarius—A New World Currency**

by Christopher P. Thompson

Copyright © 2018 by Christopher P. Thompson

Book Author by Christopher P. Thompson

Book Design by C. Ellis

ISBN—13: 978-1717289360
ISBN—10: 1717289363

# DENARIUS

## A NEW WORLD CURRENCY

### 2017-2018
### A CONCISE DENARIUS HISTORY BOOK

CHRISTOPHER P. THOMPSON

# CONTENTS

# INTRODUCTION

Since the inception of Bitcoin in 2008, thousands of cryptocurrencies or decentralised blockchains have been launched. Most ventures into the crypto sphere have not gone to plan as their founders would have hoped. Nevertheless, there are currently hundreds of crypto related projects which are succeeding.

This book covers the history of Denarius, an open source, publicly distributed cryptocurrency. It was launched on the 14th June 2017. Carsen Klock, the founder and lead developer, vowed to "follow the footsteps" of Bitcoin by implementing its core code into Denarius. He implemented the same trusted blockchain technology whilst significantly decreasing the block time for a much faster network.

Major topics covered in this book include:

- Denarius announced on Bitcointalk (JUNE 2017)

- Official Denarius forum https://denariustalk.org/ was launched (JULY 2017)

- Cryptopia exchange initiated live DNR/BTC trading (JULY 2017)

- First Denarius promotional video was published (AUGUST 2017)

- New Denarius promotional video was published (NOVEMBER 2017)

- DNR market capitalisation surpassed US$1,000,000 (DECEMBER 2017)

- DNR market capitalisation surpassed US$10,000,000 (JANUARY 2018)

- Version 2.0.0.0 wallet client updates were released (FEBRUARY 2018)

- First atomic swap occurred on the DNR Blockchain (MARCH 2018)

- Denarius was fully integrated with BarterDEX (MARCH 2018)

- Hybrid DNR Masternode payments became active (MARCH 2018)

# INTRODUCTION

To be specific, this book covers a concise chronological series of events from the 14th June 2017 to the 18th March 2018. During this time, Denarius has attracted growing interest from inside and outside the cryptocurrency space.

You may have bought this book because Denarius, DNR, is your favourite cryptographic blockchain. Alternatively, you may be keen to find out how it all began. I have presented the information henceforth without going into too much technical discussion about Denarius. If you would like to investigate further, I recommend that you read material currently available online at the official website https://denarius.io/

If you choose to purchase a certain amount of DNR, please do not buy more than you can afford to lose.

Enjoy the book :D

# WHAT IS DENARIUS?

Denarius, DNR, is a cryptocurrency or digital decentralised currency used via the Internet. It is described as a payment network without the need for a central authority such as a bank or other central clearing house. It allows the end user to store or transfer value anywhere in the world with the use of a personal computer, laptop or smartphone. Cryptography has been implemented and coded into the network allowing the user to send currency through a decentralised (no centre point of failure), open source (anyone can review the code), peer-to-peer network. Cryptography also controls the creation of newly mined/staked DNR.

Denarius is a hybrid proof of work/stake cryptocurrency based on the original Bitcoin core codebase written by Satoshi Nakamoto. Instead of adopting the hashing algorithm SHA-256, Carsen Klock, the founder and lead developer, decided to create an unique algorithm called Tribus. It consists of three of the top five NIST5 algorithms. These are called JH, Keccak and Echo. Other improvements to the original Bitcoin core codebase include stealth addresses and encrypted messaging.

The slogan used by the community to market the coin is:

## "ANCIENT MONEY FOR A NEW WORLD"

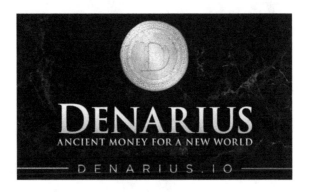

# WHY USE DENARIUS?

Like all cryptocurrencies, people have chosen to adopt Denarius as a medium of exchange/storage through personal choice.  An innovative feature of the coin, an affinity towards the brand or high confidence in the community could be reasons why they have done so.  Key  benefits of using Denarius are:

- It is a useful medium of exchange via which value can be transferred internationally for a fraction of the cost of other conventional methods.

- Denarius eliminates the need for a trusted third party such as a bank, clearing house or other centralised authority (e.g. PayPal).  All transactions are solely from one person to another (peer-to-peer).

- Denarius has the potential to engage people worldwide who are without a bank account (unbanked).

- Denarius is immune from the effects of hyperinflation, unlike the current fiat monetary systems around the world.

Carsen Klock said the following on why he called the cryptocurrency Denarius:

> "I gained inspiration for the name Denarius after the Roman currency system. The dēnārius (pronunciation: /deː.ˈnaː.rɪ.ʊs/) ; plural: dēnāriī (pronunciation: /deː.ˈnaː.rɪ.iː/) was a small silver coin first minted around 211 BC during the Second Punic War. It became the most common coin produced during ancient roman times for circulation in the general public."

Denarius markets itself as an efficient cryptocurrency, because it features faster transaction times (20x faster than Bitcoin).  It also provides users with a secure, private and reliable medium to transact, communicate and hold value.

# IS DENARIUS MONEY?

Money is a form of acceptable, convenient and valued medium of payment for goods and services within an economy. It allows two parties to exchange goods or services without the need to barter. This eradicates the potential situation where one party of the two may not want what the other has to offer. The main properties of money are:

- **As a medium of exchange**—money can be used as a means to buy/sell goods/services without the need to barter.

- **A unit of account**—a common measure of value wherever one is in the world.

- **Portable**—easily transferred from one party to another. The medium used can be easily carried.

- **Durable**—all units of the currency can be lost, but not destroyed.

- **Divisible**—each unit can be subdivided into smaller fractions of that unit.

- **Fungible**— each unit of account is the same as every other unit within the medium (1 DNR = 1 DNR).

- **As a store of value**—it sustains its purchasing power (what it can buy) over long periods of time.

Denarius easily satisfies the first six characteristics. Taking into account the last characteristic, the value of Denarius, like all currencies, comes from people willing to accept it as a medium of exchange for payment of goods or services. Additionally, it must be a secure way to store personal wealth. As it gets adopted by more individuals or merchants, its intrinsic value will increase accordingly.

# COIN SPECIFICATION

At the time of publication of this book, its specification is:

| | |
|---|---|
| **Unit of Account:** | DNR |
| **Time of Original Launch:** | 14th June 2017 at 22:23:38 UTC |
| **Time of Announcement:** | 14th June 2017 at 22:43:49 UTC |
| **Founder/Lead Developer:** | Carsen Klock |
| **Hashing Algorithm:** | Tribus (consists of JH, Keccak and Echo) |
| **Timestamping Algorithm:** | Hybrid PoW/PoS (for the 1st 3 years) |
| **Total Coins:** | 10,000,000 DNR |
| **Number of Confirmations:** | 10, maturity: 30 |
| **Block Time:** | 30 seconds |
| **Block Reward:** | (see page 19) |
| **Masternodes:** | (see page 17) |
| **Pre-mine:** | 1,000,000 DNR |

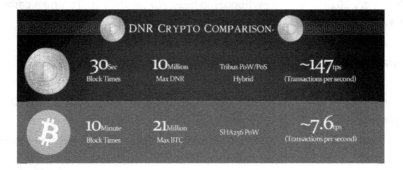

# MILESTONE TIMELINE

| | |
|---|---|
| **14th June 2017** | —First block timestamped at 22:23:38 UTC |
| **14th June 2017** | —Announced on Bitcointalk at 22:43:49 UTC |
| **15th June 2017** | —Official Denarius website launched |
| **15th June 2017** | —First exchange to initiate DNR/BTC was CoinsMarkets |
| **2nd July 2017** | —DNR added to www.coinmarketcap.com |
| **5th July 2017** | —Version 1.0.1.0 wallet client update released |
| **10th July 2017** | —Version 1.0.2.0 wallet client update released |
| **12th July 2017** | —Official forum https://denariustalk.org/ went live |
| **17th July 2017** | —Version 1.0.3.0 wallet client update released |
| **21st July 2017** | —Cryptopia initiated the DNR/BTC trading pair |
| **31st July 2017** | —Version 1.0.4.0 wallet client update released |
| **19th August 2017** | —Version 1.0.5.0 wallet client update released |
| **26th August 2017** | —First DNR promotional video published |
| **5th September 2017** | —Version 1.0.6.0 wallet client update released |
| **7th October 2017** | —Version 1.0.7.0 wallet client update released |
| **30th November 2017** | —New DNR promotional video published |
| **1st December 2017** | —DNR market capitalisation surpassed US$1,000,000 |
| **1st January 2018** | —DNR market capitalisation surpassed US$10,000,000 |
| **10th January 2018** | —Whopper.io began to sell DNR Cold Storage Cards |
| **24th February 2018** | —Version 2.0.0.0 wallet client update released |
| **3rd March 2018** | —Version 2.0.1.0 wallet client update released |
| **4th March 2018** | —Version 2.0.2.0 wallet client update released |
| **4th March 2018** | —First atomic swap occurred on the DNR Blockchain |
| **10th March 2018** | —DNR fully integrated with decentralised BarterDEX |
| **17th March 2018** | —Version 2.0.5.0 wallet client update released |
| **18th March 2018** | —Hybrid DNR Masternode payments became active |

# CORE FEATURES

Denarius is officially described as possessing the following core features:

**Secure** —censorship, fraud and third party interference do not exist.

**Fast** —transactions take about 5 minutes to fully confirm.

**Reliable** —the secure decentralised consensus method PoW/PoS sustains a network without risk of downtime.

**Stealth Addresses** —users can send DNR units of account securely and privately.

**Encrypted Messaging** —users can communicate via the Denarius network to and from public or stealth addresses.

**Multi-Signature** —multi-signature addresses require two or more users to authorise a transaction.

**Hybrid Masternodes** —following the release of version 2.0.0.0 on the 24th February 2018, users were able to form Masternodes, MN, that cost 5,000 DNR each to keep active. They provide the holder 33% of block rewards. More information can be found on page 17.

**Cross-Chain Atomic Swaps** —a decentralised exchange called BarterDEX can be used to trade DNR units of account with other accepted cryptocurrencies, assets or tokens without the need for a trusted third party (centralised exchange).

# BLOCKCHAIN

Every cryptocurrency has a corresponding blockchain within its decentralised network protocol. Denarius is no different in this sense. A blockchain is simply described as a general public ledger of all transactions and blocks ever executed since the very first block. In addition, it continuously updates in real time each time a new block is successfully mined. Blocks enter the blockchain in such a manner that each block contains the hash of the previous one. It is therefore utterly resistant to modification along the chain since each block is related to the prior one. Consequently, the problem of doubling-spending is solved.

Block number one of the Denarius Blockchain timestamped at 22:23:38 UTC on the 14th June 2017. The first atomic swap happened on the DNR Blockchain on the 4th March 2018.

As a means for members of the general public to view the blockchain, web developers have designed and created block explorers. They tend to present different layouts, statistics and charts. Some explorers are more extensive in terms of the information given. Usual statistics included are:

- **Height of block**        —the block number of the network.

- **Time of block**          —the time at which the block was timestamped to the blockchain.

- **Transactions**           —the number of transactions in that particular block.

- **Total Sent**             —the total amount of cryptocurrency sent in that particular block.

- **Block Reward**           —how many coins were generated in the block (added to the overall coin circulation).

# MASTERNODES

A masternode, MN, is basically a full node or computer that stores, in real time, a full copy of the blockchain. This is similar to all other known nodes in other cryptocurrencies. Besides this common characteristic, they also perform other functions some of which are:

- They help increase the privacy/anonymity of transactions.

- They enable instant transactions.

- They allow the MN holder to participate in democratic processes.

Masternodes can be run by anyone, but there is an entry barrier. The MN holder has something at stake, so is not inclined to cheat the system. In the case of Denarius, DNR Hybrid Masternode holders must store a minimum of 5,000 DNR in a designated MN wallet address. The holder must also possess a stable IP address and have sufficient storage space on their computer to store the full blockchain.

Since the 18th March 2018, DNR Hybrid Masternode holders receive 33% of all DNR units of account generated via PoW and PoS.

**Carsen Klock**
@carsenk

Follow

$DNR Block 645k has passed successfully and masternode payments have now started!!! #masternodes #hybrid #blockchain #cryptocurrency #alts #altcoins $crypto $btc $ltc $dash

1:27 AM - 18 Mar 2018

14 Retweets 44 Likes

# PROOF OF WORK/STAKE

Both proof of work and proof of stake are used by Denarius as timestamping methods. They secure the distributed consensus mechanism in order to sustain and validate transactions. Therefore, no third party entity is required, or needs to be trusted, to verify, and then add transactions to the DNR Blockchain.

During proof of work mining, miners use computer processing power (hashrate) to secure the network by competing for high difficulty hashes. Miners who successfully find a block, individually or collectively on a mining pool, are rewarded DNR units of account (block reward and transaction fees) as an incentive. Proof of work mining for Denarius will end in May 2020 after an anticipated 3,000,000 blocks (70% of which are PoW blocks) have been timestamped.

Proof of stake, on the other hand, allows DNR wallet users to receive a DNR stake by keeping their client connected to the network. Stakers are only required to use low difficulty hashes to receive transaction fees found in a particular PoS block. As soon as Denarius transitions to full PoS, stakers will receive 6% nominal interest.

## PoW BLOCK REWARD STRUCTURE

```
            if (pindexBest->nHeight == 1)
        nSubsidy = 1000000 * COIN;  // 10% Premine
else if (pindexBest->nHeight <= FAIR_LAUNCH_BLOCK) // Block 210, Instamine prevention
                nSubsidy = 1 * COIN/2;
    else if (pindexBest->nHeight <= 1000000) // Block 1m ~ 3m DNR
                nSubsidy = 3 * COIN;
    else if (pindexBest->nHeight <= 2000000) // Block 2m ~ 4m DNR
                nSubsidy = 4 * COIN;
    else if (pindexBest->nHeight <= 3000000) // Block 3m ~ 3m DNR
                nSubsidy = 3 * COIN;
      else if (pindexBest->nHeight > LAST_POW_BLOCK) // Block 3m
                nSubsidy = 0;  // PoW Ends
```

## PoS BLOCK REWARD STRUCTURE

```
nCoinAge * 0.06 / 365;
```

# DNR BLOCKS

Each and every time a miner successfully finds a block, they are eligible to receive a reward for their effort. This happens, on average, every 30 seconds on the DNR Blockchain. Those who mine DNR units of account during the three year hybrid PoW/PoS phase can receive 3 or 4 DNR (see table below) as an incentive. On the other hand, wallet client users who keep their DNR clients open and running on their computers (stakers), receive a relatively small amount via PoS.

A quote from the DNR Whitescroll (Whitepaper aka. Technical Paper) is:

> "Even if the difficulty of the PoW blocks increases significantly, blocks that are full of transactions can still be processed by PoS miners at a low difficulty to ensure that even at times of very high PoW difficulty, block times can remain at or below 30 seconds."

A pre-mine was created at block number two on the 14th June 2017 at 22:24:03 UTC. It was split 50/50 to fund different areas of the project. One half was dedicated towards bounties and marketing costs for the first 6-12 months, whereas the other half is being used for development costs over the lifetime of the project.

What follows is an outlined block reward distribution table:

| YEAR | BLOCK NUMBER | BLOCK REWARD | TOTAL (excl max PoS of 30%) |
|------|--------------|--------------|------------------------------|
| 1 | 1 | 0.5 | 0.5 |
| 1 | 2 | 1,000,000 | 1,000,000 |
| 1 | 3-211 | 0.5 | 104.5 |
| 1 | 212-1,000,000 | 3 | 2,100,000 |
| 2 | 1,000,001-2,000,000 | 4 | 2,800,000 |
| 3 | 2,000,001-3,000,000 | 3 | 2,100,000 |

It is predicted that there will be approximately 8,000,000 DNR at the end of the PoW mining phase (May 2020).

# WALLET CLIENTS

A wallet client is basically software used on a personal computer, smartphone or tablet which allows a user to execute transfers of cryptocurrency. Alternatively, it can be described as a means to access coins from the inseparable blockchain (public transaction ledger). The wallet cryptographically generates and holds the public and private keys necessary to make transactions possible.

Lead developer Carsen Klock has developed the necessary source code and released regular wallet client updates, especially for the Windows operating system. All wallet release notes can be found on pages 52 to 62 or online at https://github.com/carsenk/denarius/releases.

What follows are the main DNR wallets available to the public:

- Core QT wallet clients (Windows and Mac OS X)

- Coinomi Android wallet

- Agama wallets (Windows and Mac)

# CRYPTOCURRENCY EXCHANGES

A cryptocurrency exchange offers its users a service which can be used to buy and sell DNR units of account on an active trading platform. They also determine the price of one unit of DNR account denominated in terms of Bitcoin, and hence the overall DNR market capitalisation.

As well as the initiation of DNR on centralised exchanges, it was fully integrated with the decentralised exchange called BarterDEX on the 10th March 2018.

Denarius trading has been initiated on numerous exchanges. According to www.coinmarketcap.com, the vast majority of trades occur on the centralised exchange called Cryptopia. Other exchanges which offer DNR/BTC trading are:

| DATE DNR TRADING INITIATED | EXCHANGE | TRADING STATUS |
| ---: | :---: | :---: |
| 15th June 2017 | CoinsMarkets | |
| 19th June 2017 | CryptoDAO Limited | |
| 29th June 2017 | Novaexchange | |
| 29th June 2017 | CoinExchange | ACTIVE |
| 20th August 2017 | TradeSatoshi | |
| 21st July 2017 | Cryptopia | ACTIVE |
| 16th November 2017 | Stocks.exchange | ACTIVE |
| 29th January 2018 | SouthXchange | ACTIVE |
| 10th March 2018 | BarterDEX | ACTIVE |

*

# COMMUNITY

A community is a social unit or network that shares common values and goals. It derives from the old French word "comuntee". This, in turn, originates from "communitas" in Latin (communis; things held in common). Denarius has a community consisting of an innumerable number of people who have the coin's wellbeing and future goal at heart. The majority of these people prefer fictitious names with optional avatars.

Carsen Klock is the founder and lead developer of the Denarius project. He is dedicated to making it a great success by developing innovative features and expanding its vision. Other developers also help drive Denarius forward.

At the time of publication, there are social media sites (and other official websites) on which discussion and development of Denarius take place. The community spend most of their time communicating on their official Discord channel. Other major websites include:

- https://denarius.io/                                    Official Website
- https://denariustalk.org/                               Official Forum
- https://twitter.com/denariuscoin                        Twitter Account
- https://gitter.im/denariusproject/Lobby                 Gitter Channel
- https://bitcointalk.org/index.php?topic=1967207.0       Bitcointalk Thread

In essence, the community surrounding and participating in the development of Denarius is the backbone of the coin. Without a following, the prospects of future adoption and utilisation are starkly limited. Denarius belongs to all those who use it, not just to the developers who aid its progression.

# A CONCISE HISTORY OF DENARIUS

## LIST OF CHAPTERS

I.      **DENARIUS ANNOUNCED ON BITCOINTALK ON 14TH JUNE 2017**

II.      **OFFICIAL DENARIUS FORUM LAUNCHED ON 12TH JULY 2017**

III.      **CAMPAIGNS WERE LAUNCHED TO SPREAD DNR AWARENESS**

IV.      **CORE QT WALLET CLIENTS REGULARLY POSTED BY CARSEN KLOCK**

V.      **DNR ACTIVE TRADING BEGAN ON SEVERAL EXCHANGES**

# 1

# DENARIUS ANNOUNCED ON BITCOINTALK

*"Yes I am in for the long haul and will be developing the coin and other awesome open source software."* - Carsen Klock

As a way to announce Denarius to the wider cryptocurrency community, an official Bitcointalk forum thread was created on the 14th June 2017 at 22:43:49 UTC. It was titled "[ANN] Denarius [DNR] - New "Tribus" PoW Algo >> Ancient Money For a New World!".  Carsen Klock, the founder and lead developer, had fulfilled his promise to create a decentralised and open source  cryptocurrency.  He made a vow to devote himself to Denarius.

Carsen Klock notified initial followers that wallet client and source code releases would be posted at https://github.com/carsenk/denarius/releases and all relevant trusted links would be promptly posted.  He was also eager for people to translate the opening post of the official Denarius Bitcointalk forum thread into other languages besides English.  Each genuine translation would be rewarded 1,000 DNR.

**Block #1 (Reward 0.5 DNR) June 14th 2017 at 10:23:38 PM UTC**

**Block #2 (Reward 1,000,000 DNR) June 14th 2017 at 10:24:03 PM UTC**

As can be seen above, the first block timestamped to the DNR Blockchain roughly twenty minutes before Denarius was announced. Block number two generated the 1,000,000 DNR pre-mine to be used for giveaways, competitions and overall development. From the beginning, the timestamping algorithm was hybrid proof of work/stake (PoW/PoS).

Also on the 14th June, the first wallet client was released. Carsen Klock posted relevant download links on GitHub. Besides this, Bitcointalk forum user "ex_mac" announced that the first Denarius Block Explorer had been launched at https://lpool.name/explorer/DNR.

At block number 212, the reward per PoW block increased from 0.5 DNR to 3 DNR:

**Block #211 (Reward 0.5 DNR) June 15th 2017 at 12:41:57 AM UTC**

**Block #212 (Reward 3.0 DNR) June 15th 2017 at 12:42:05 AM UTC**

During the days which followed, several social media accounts, discussion channels and other websites were launched. These included:

- On the 15th June, https://denarius.io (Official Website)

- On the 15th June, https://twitter.com/denariuscoin (@denariuscoin)

- On the 15th June, https://chainz.cryptoid.info/dnr (Block Explorer)

- On the 15th June, https://gitter.im/denariusproject/Lobby

- On the 16th June, https://denarius.slack.com

- On the 17th June, https://www.reddit.com/r/denariuscoin

On the 15th June, the first cryptocurrency exchange platform initiated live DNR/BTC trading at https://coinsmarkets.com/trade-BTC-DNR.htm. CoinsMarkets is a small and obscure exchange. Denarius is no longer recognised as being active there.

On the 19th June, the second cryptocurrency exchange called CryptoDAO Limited initiated five DNR related trading pairs. CryptoDAO Limited is no longer recognised as offering its users DNR trading.

Despite the addition to two exchanges, the community were eager to attract the attention of more reputable exchanges. YoBit, Bittrex and Poloniex were suggested as possible options.

On the 28th June, two campaigns designed to increase the awareness of Denarius across the wider cryptocurrency community and beyond began. These were:

- **Signature Campaign**—rewards were given to participants on a weekly basis for posting comments on the Bitcointalk forum besides a related Denarius Signature. The signature would be different based on the forum user's rank. Bonuses for loyalty and following the rules existed. User "iluvbitcoins" was hired to manage it.

- **Twitter Campaign**—Twitter users had to retweet at least three tweets from the accounts @denariuscoin or @carsenjk and post one tweet including the @denariuscoin or @carsenjk mention with $DNR or $crypto. Accounts which had more followers were eligible for a greater reward. For instance, an account with more than 10,000 followers could claim 50 DNR.

There were numerous requests for the addition of Denarius to other exchanges besides CoinsMarkets and CryptoDAO Limited. Carsen Klock was understandably reluctant to pay the immense fees some exchanges required for Denarius to be added promptly. Other members of the community were more patient and cautious. They argued that if Denarius deserved to be added to more reputable exchanges, demand via DNR trading volume would warrant it.

On the 29th June, two cryptocurrency exchanges initiated live DNR trading:

- Novaexchange:      https://novaexchange.com/market/BTC_DNR/
- CoinExchange:      https://www.coinexchange.io/market/DNR/BTC/

On the 2nd July, after innumerable requests from Carsen Klock and other members of the community, Denarius was added to www.coinmarketcap.com. It primarily ranks hundreds of cryptocurrencies, decentralised assets and tokens in descending order of market capitalisation. Other statistics are also accessible from there.

The first recorded DNR market capitalisation on www.coinmarketcap.com was US$15,646 on the 2nd July. At this opening figure, the corresponding prices per unit of DNR account were US$0.170773 and 7,114 Bitcoin Satoshi. As shown below, the market capitalisation surpassed US$100,000 on the 6th July. At this time, no pre-mined DNR units of account were included in the overall coin circulation.

|  | Low US$ | Open US$ | Close US$ | High US$ | Volume US$ | Market Cap US$ |
|---|---|---|---|---|---|---|
| 2nd July | 0.169813 | 0.170773 | 0.245451 | 0.268524 | 11,085 | 15,647 |
| 3rd July | 0.219950 | 0.244547 | 0.297499 | 0.344013 | 14,172 | 23,647 |
| 4th July | 0.268083 | 0.296823 | 0.479293 | 0.831678 | 32,611 | 30,271 |
| 5th July | 0.424812 | 0.479034 | 0.920160 | 0.943574 | 38,608 | 51,373 |
| 6th July | 0.667284 | 0.930137 | 1.57 | 1.85 | 76,749 | 104,815 |

On the 6th July, according to historical charts available at www.coinmarketcap.com, the price of each and every DNR unit of account surpassed US$1 for the first time:

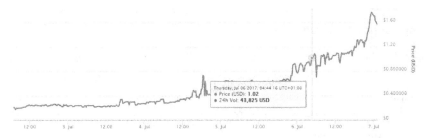

Carsen Klock advised users trading DNR on CoinsMarkets to be very careful. There had been reports of dubious activity there. Instead, he recommended traders to use either CoinExchange or Novaexchange. He was also quoted as saying:

> "Yes I am in for the long haul and will be developing
>
> the coin and other awesome open source software 😎 (like the NodeJS Web Wallet, maybe a new NodeJS Block Explorer etc.)"

On the 7th July, Carsen Klock was happy to disclose information about the pre-mined DNR units of account balance. It stood at approximately 675,000 DNR. This obviously meant that 325,000 DNR had already been used to pay for bounties, giveaways, external services and other related campaigns.

On the 12th July, the https://denariustalk.org/ forum went live. There were minor issues with some people being unable to access it after they had registered, but they were easily fixed. Over 100 members registered within the first 24 hours. It serves as a platform for discussing development, mining, marketing and so on.

Also on this day, the first giveaway on the official Denarius forum happened. It simply required members to post their DNR wallet address to receive 1 DNR. It was limited to the first 100 posts on the giveaway thread.

Two days later, after the success of the first giveaway, a second giveaway thread was created on the same forum. It was open to 500 members this time. Both giveaways were limited to one post per person.

On the 18th July 2017, a campaign was launched to get Denarius actively trading on the Cryptopia exchange platform. A 1.1 BTC or 200,000 DOT fee was required for this to be possible. It took less than one day to achieve this fee and, as a result, the listing was paid for and then submitted.

Three days later, Cryptopia initiated live DNR/BTC trading. It is an exchange (as well as a marketplace and forum) based in New Zealand which offers deposits, withdraws and trades of Bitcoin, Litecoin, and over 400 other cryptocurrencies. It went live on the 6th December 2014. Denarius has enjoyed the vast majority of trades on this exchange.

During July, four core QT wallet client release updates were posted by Carsen Klock at https://github.com/carsenk/denarius/releases/. These were:

- Windows version 1.0.1.0 on the 5th July. Small updates had been made to kernels and keys. It was not described as a mandatory update.

- Windows version 1.0.2.0 on the 10th July. It introduced a "Market" tab that displays the values of DNR/BTC, BTC/USD and the DNR market capitalisation. Carsen Klock admitted it was "a bit rough around the edges", but promised to "smooth it out" in the next release.

- Windows version 1.0.3.0 on the 17th July. Further updates were made to the "Market" tab display. The "About Dialogue" box was also amended. It was described as a small update.

- Windows version 1.0.4.0 on the 31st July. It introduced a new USD balance figure on the overview page. Several technical fixes were also made.

Versions for Mac OS X followed each release update above within a day or two. Version 1.0.4.0 for Mac OS X was released on the 5th August 2017.

On the 9th August, an article relating to Denarius was published on a "Crypo, Finance and Tech News" website called "The Merkle" (founded in June 2014). It was titled "Crypto vs VISA—Can Denarius Compete When It Comes To Transactions Per Second?" and written by James Woods. It said the following about Denarius:

"So how fast is Denarius? Denarius is able to handle about 147 transactions per second! Over 20 times faster than Bitcoin and twice as fast as Bitcoin Cash. Denarius sets the standard higher for transaction speeds on a blockchain. You can find more information about Denarius at https://denarius.io"

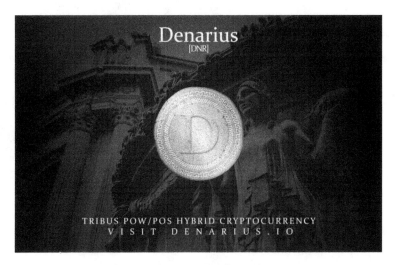

Two more core QT wallet client updates were released in Summer 2017:

- Windows version 1.0.5.0 on the 19th August. It added a "BTC Total" figure to the overview page. It is calculated by multiplying the user's total held DNR units of account by the current Bitcoin price per DNR unit of account. Other cosmetic changes had been made to the user interface. A Mac OS X wallet client was released on the following day.

- Windows version 1.0.6.0 on the 5th September. It incorporated a new "Staking" tab. It gives an estimation of a user's stake, but was still in its very early development phase. Three technical RPC commands were also added for users. These were *createmultisig*, *gethashespersec* and *dumpbootstrap*.

During Summer 2017, the DNR market capitalisation attained all time highs on several occasions. From the 27th July to the 14th September, it more than doubled from US$290,567 to US$664,055 according to www.coinmarketcap.com.

What follows is a table of Bitcoin Satoshi prices per unit of DNR account on Cryptopia over the aforementioned period. It also shows the corresponding daily 24 hour DNR volumes on that exchange.

| | Low | Open | Close | High | Volume DNR |
|---|---|---|---|---|---|
| 27th July 2017 | 20,000 | 24,130 | 22,020 | 28,990 | 10,812.82 |
| 3rd August 2017 | 13,270 | 15,800 | 15,200 | 19,710 | 6,263.30 |
| 10th August 2017 | 20,010 | 20,860 | 21,850 | 24,470 | 8,688.97 |
| 17th August 2017 | 10,330 | 15,000 | 12,500 | 15,010 | 10,203.35 |
| 24th August 2017 | 12,800 | 14,000 | 12,800 | 14,830 | 8,870.79 |
| 31st August 2017 | 11,240 | 11,240 | 12,700 | 13,332 | 23,537.16 |
| 7th September 2017 | 11,200 | 11,260 | 11,720 | 12,140 | 8,857.51 |
| 14th September 2017 | 10,800 | 11,500 | 10,800 | 12,000 | 15,794.54 |

**SOURCE: www.cryptocompare.com**

Two charts below show how the market capitalisation and US Dollar price of one unit of DNR account (1 DNR) had fluctuated since the 2nd July 2017:

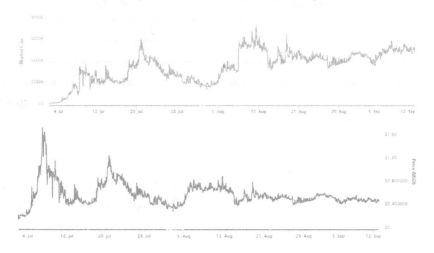

Other events which occurred during this period included:

- The first proof of stake block timestamped to the DNR Blockchain on the 15th June 2017 at 15:27:56 UTC.

- On the 16th June, user "bumbacoin" posted the first Mac OS X wallet client release. He received a bounty for his work four days later.

- On the 22nd June, the first DNR faucet went live at leakyfaucet.info.

- On the 26th June, a tipping bot debuted on the Denarius Gitter Channel. User "enkayz" was praised for creating it.

- The first news article written about Denarius was published by @VikingChild at http://cryptovore.com/2017/07/02/what-is-denarius-and-gpu-mining-hashrate/

- On the 21st July, DNR was added to the Coinomi Android Wallet App. Coinomi have offered secure wallets for Bitcoin and other coins since 2014.

- On the 22nd July, the Denarius Whitepaper (Whitescroll) was published at http://denarius.io/whitescroll.pdf. Future amendments were not ruled out.

- On the 20th August, an exchange called TradeSatoshi initiated live DNR trading at https://www.tradesatoshi.com/Exchange?market=DNR_BTC.

- On the 26th August, the first Denarius promotional video was uploaded to YouTube titled "What is Denarius?". Four screenshots are visible below:

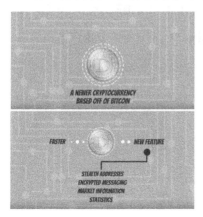

I.     VERSION 1.0.7.0 WALLET CLIENT UPDATES RELEASED

II.     BRAND NEW DNR PROMOTIONAL VIDEO PUBLISHED

III.     DNR MARKET CAPITALISATION SURPASSED US$1,000,0000

IV.     SIX MONTH ANNIVERSARY CELEBRATED

V.     CARSEN KLOCK INTERVIEWED

# 2

---

# FURTHER PROMOTION
# AND ADOPTION

*"A Denarius has always been something of interest to me, the story behind them,
their age and rarity.  Making a crypto with another name of "Somethingcoin" was not
in my vocabulary.  I wanted something unique and valuable sounding.
Denarius it is." - Carsen Klock*

Carsen Klock was happy about how stable Denarius had been, especially in terms of the underlying code.  He also emphasised the price stability.  One unit of DNR account had been more or less US$0.50 for quite a while.  He reiterated his commitment to the project and promised to carry on fixing and adding new features.  In particular, he was proud of the multi-signature support added in latest version (v1.0.6.0) on the 5th September 2017.

In terms of the number of units of DNR account in circulation, he said:

**"The pre-mine is not large anymore by any means, I only hold
400k now and there is already around 1m DNR in circulation currently, so
it's less than half of what is available now."**

Further promotions, giveaways and contests were planned in the near future.

There were unsurprisingly some people who thought proof of stake timestamping was not operational. Carsen Klock stated that it had always been active. At the time, there were more PoW blocks than PoS blocks being timestamped.

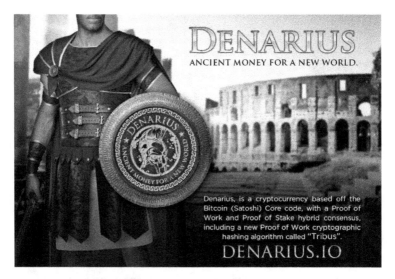

On the 7th October, an expected update to the wallet client software was released. It was version 1.0.7.0 and it included many miscellaneous fixes and other changes:

- Fixes to the graphical user interface (GUI).

- Updated TX icons.

- Staking estimation TAB changes.

- Fixed Display of market values e.g. USD Balance.

Members of the community described the transition to version 1.0.7.0 (see page 56) as smooth. It was not a mandatory update, but highly recommended.

On the 31st October, the last recorded October DNR market capitalisation according to the website www.coinmarketcap.com was approx. US$402,756. Corresponding values per unit of DNR account were US$0.228656 and 3,579 Bitcoin Satoshi. This meant there were roughly 1,761,405 DNR in circulation.

On the 16th November, it was announced that live DNR/BTC trading had begun on Stocks.exchange at https://stocks.exchange/trade/DNR/BTC. This exchange had only just been launched. Carsen Klock described it initially as being reliable.

On the last day of November, Carsen Klock was proud to present a new Denarius promotional video. BlocStart Solutions (@BlocStart on Twitter) were credited for producing it. Two screenshots are shown above. The community were encouraged to share it. It is titled "What is Denarius Coin?" and can be found at:

**https://www.youtube.com/watch?v=Z1T1q4Nm5uk**

Another event on the 30th November concerned the official Denarius website. It had been revamped to look, as Bitcointalk user "Elder III" said, very clean, sharp and informative. Carsen Klock concurred with what he said.

On the following day, the DNR market capitalisation surpassed US$1,000,000 for the first time ever. Historical data derived from www.coinmarketcap.com is:

| | Low US$ | Open US$ | Close US$ | High US$ | 1 DNR US$ | Market Cap US$ |
|---|---|---|---|---|---|---|
| 1st Dec | 0.323796 | 0.334893 | 0.747685 | 0.788733 | 0.533157 | 1,023,913 |

On the 14th December, Carsen Klock pointed out that it had been six months since the DNR Blockchain launched. He stated over 250,000 transactions had occurred on the DNR Blockchain so far. There were no recent major problems to report concerning, as he described, the robust and functional blockchain.

Once block number 443,702 timestamped, the DNR Blockchain was six months old:

Block #443,702 (Reward 0 DNR) December 14th 2017 at 10:24:50 PM UTC

To celebrate the six month anniversary, http://btfd.shop/ hosted a giveaway. Twitter users had to retweet and like a specific tweet to have a chance to win DNR related merchandise (see below).

On the following day, a random tweet generator selected two winners of the above giveaway. They were @JustUsMining and @CryptoBuc.

Two days later, the total number of DNR units of account generated surpassed two million. This resulted from the timestamp of block number 446,004:

Block #446,004 (Reward 3.0 DNR) December 16th 2017 at 01:04:33 AM UTC

On the 18th December, an introductory Q&A with Carsen Klock was published at https://medium.com/@Panama_TJ/denarius-intro-504ba3f16728. Nine questions were asked and answered:

### Question 1—Tell us about your crypto developer background.

My name is Carsen Klock. I have been in crypto since very early on, around 2013 and 2014. I created a plethora of altcoins during the altcoin rush. Most of my cryptos were experiments and tests to learn more about blockchains and how the ecosystem/community worked around these cryptos. After a lot of backlash, I got hired at GAW Miners as their Lead Front-End Developer. Shortly after the collapse of GAW and loss of my position, I got hired at Apple where I worked for the past few years, finally realizing that not even at Apple was where I belong, I wanted to get back into crypto full-time, so thats where my project Denarius comes in at.

### Question 2—Why DNR?

A Denarius has always been something of interest to me, the story behind them, their age and rarity. Making a crypto with another name of "Somethingcoin" was not in my vocabulary. I wanted something unique and valuable sounding, Denarius it is.

### Question 3—DNR specs and how this translates to English for non-crypto speakers?

DNR features 147 tps, 30 second blocks, 10 Million Max Coins, MultiSig Transactions and Addresses, Stealth Addresses, Encrypted Messaging, and a new unique PoW algorithm I created called "Tribus".

SPECIFICATIONS

Denarius is a new cryptocurrency based off the original Bitcoin Core by Satoshi Nakamoto. Denarius features many changes, such as Stealth Addresses, Encrypted Messaging, Multi-Signature Support, Tribus a brand new PoW hashing algorithm that is ASIC resistant, and a max of 10,000,000 DNR to be created during the PoW lifecycle of 3 years, which then transitions entirely to Proof of Stake.

10,000,000 DNR Max

10% Premine of 1,000,000 DNR
50% of the premine 500,000 DNR will be going to bounties, promotions, marketing, and services.
The other 50% is my personal funding for maintaining and funding the development of this coin.
(As of 9/12/2017 I hold only around 400k DNR out of the original 1m premine)
(As of 9/25/2017, CoinMarketCap included the entire premine of 1m into the current supply in circulation.)

30 second block times
10 Confirmations
30 Confirmations to mature blocks
Tribus Proof-of-Work Hashing Algorithm featuring 3 of the top NIST5 algos (JH, Keccak, and Echo)
Proof-of-Stake Hybrid which will fully transition to PoS which PoW ends on block 3,000,000
Multi-Signature Support in Wallet and RPC
Staking Estimation Tab showing estimated staking probability of staking and DNR reward
Block Explorer in Wallet
Statistics Tab in Wallet showing almost all of Denarius's data
Market Information Tab in Wallet showing market data of DNR and BTC

### Question 4—Why DNR is unique, and why it will thrive?

DNR is unique in the aspect of it being a Hybrid crypto, which is not common. It also features the exclusive Tribus Proof-Of-Work Algorithm and Multisig Support natively in the wallet. The max amount of DNR that will ever be available is much less and more rare than many many other coins. The Denarius QT wallet is also fairly unique in the sea of altcoins as we have market information native in the wallet, a block explorer, statistics, and more!

### Question 5—How different is DNR from your closest competitor?

DNR is usually much faster and more rare than its competitors and it can generally handle a much higher transaction per second rate. For example, Litecoin can only handle 26 tps or Ethereum at 15 tps vs. Denarius's 147 tps. (tps: transactions per second).

### Question 6—What lays ahead in the short/long term for DNR?

Development updates. More external services/markets/exchanges/etc.

### Question 7—What is/will be DNR marketing plan? Funding?

Denarius does not really have any set plans or funding as it is a decentralized cryptocurrency, there is no company or person backing Denarius, it is simply powered by the people and our community. We do generally do paid advertising for Denarius on Facebook, Instagram, and Twitter.

### Question 8—Plans for other exchanges?

Well, there is always plans for other exchanges, as far as those centralized exchanges getting in contact or being outstanding at customer service, most are lacking in this regard, Crypto developers are commonly ignored/mistreated/etc. by centralized exchanges (Bittrex, Poloniex, Binance, HitBTC, Bit-Z etc.). These exchanges over the years have only gotten more greedy and generally require a very hefty fee to be listed (Some are upwards of $200,000 USD or 9 BTC), which takes them maybe a few minutes of work, and is not something I support at all. We do hope to do some development updates in the future to Denarius to further support gettxout RPC commands and BIP 65 (Bitcoin Improvement Proposal 65) to allow Alice/Bob support of Atomic Swaps with the new BarterDEX by KMD. DEXs are the future of exchanges and we hope to see Denarius on more of them!

**Question 9—What will the roadmap look like after 2018?**

We do not have a roadmap as we are not an ICO, corporation, company, etc. I am working on Denarius in my free-time, by myself generally, so development comes as it will... Masternodes have been talked about within the community and much of the community has shown support for these. I have started to develop the masternode code in the Denarius branch called "masternodes", currently if we are able to get them integrated on chain, the cost of a masternode will be 5,000 DNR and a 33% block reward. The more developers/help/testers I get on board with Denarius, the faster new features and ideas can come to life.

On the 23rd December, Carsen Klock was ecstatic about what he had received through the mail. He was quoted as saying:

> "I just got my hands on some $DNR Cold Storage Cards, they are prime!
> @Elypse_Pink @WhopperCrypto @denariuscoin #blockchain $crypto I will be
> giving a few of these away every week for the next few months! First giveaway
> will be Dec 29th. Simply retweet this and good luck!!!"

Other events which occurred during this period included:

- On the 21st October, direct trading between Denarius and Ethereum became active on CoinExchange.io.

- On the 22nd October, the official Denarius Telegram Group was created.

- On the 29th October, an online Twitter bot @denariibot went live. It allows users to tip each other DNR units of account on Twitter.

- On the 4th December, a new Chrome Extension for displaying the price per DNR was posted at https://github.com/carsenk/simple-denarius-ticker.

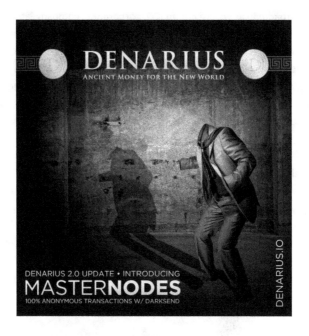

I.  DNR MARKET CAPITALISATION SURPASSED US$10,000,000

II.  DNR WHOPPER STORAGE CARDS AVAILABLE TO PURCHASE

III.  VERSION 2.0 WALLET CLIENT RELEASED ON 24TH FEBRUARY 2018

IV.  FIRST ATOMIC SWAP OCCURRED ON THE DNR BLOCKCHAIN

V.  MASTERNODE PAYMENTS BEGAN ON 18TH MARCH 2018

# 3

# TRANSITION TO
# MASTERNODE TECHNOLOGY

*"Yup we just passed block 645k and masternode payments have started!"* - Carsen Klock

A growing number of people had discovered cryptocurrency and blockchain technology during 2017. Most popular blockchains such as Bitcoin, Ethereum etc. had gained more media attention than ever before. Denarius had also gained more support as evident in the number of followers on Twitter and other social media platforms. On the 1st January 2018, the following, including Denarius, were some of the top cryptocurrencies in terms of market capitalisation:

| | Low US$ | Open US$ | Close US$ | High US$ | Market Cap US$ |
|---|---|---|---|---|---|
| Bitcoin | 13,154.70 | 14,112.20 | 13,637.20 | 14,112.20 | 236,725,000,000 |
| Ethereum | 742.00 | 755.76 | 772.64 | 782.53 | 73,075,800,000 |
| Bitcoin Cash | 2,389.52 | 2,534.82 | 2,432.54 | 2,534.86 | 42,804,800,000 |
| Denarius | 2.99 | 3.07 | 3.42 | 5.01 | 6,397,520 |

Not long after the all time high 2017 market capitalisation was attained on the 31st December, it went on to surpass US$10,000,000 for the first time on New Years Day 2018. According to www.coinmarketcap.com, a peak at US$10,408,827 was reached with corresponding values of one unit of DNR account at US$5.01 and 36,923 Bitcoin Satoshi (the highest BTC Satoshi value since the 21st July 2017).

What follows are historical figures derived from www.coinmarketcap.com:

|  | Low US$ | Open US$ | Close US$ | High US$ | Volume US$ | Market Cap US$ |
|---|---|---|---|---|---|---|
| 28th Dec | 0.750477 | 0.912257 | 1.02 | 1.08 | 25,654 | 1,880,610 |
| 29th Dec | 1.03 | 1.03 | 1.81 | 1.94 | 189,332 | 2,127,750 |
| 30th Dec | 1.36 | 1.81 | 1.92 | 1.95 | 175,897 | 3,752,040 |
| 31st Dec | 1.72 | 1.90 | 3.14 | 3.14 | 147,206 | 3,939,880 |
| 1st Jan | 2.99 | 3.07 | 3.542 | 5.01 | 471,336 | 6,397,520 |

It was the first time the 24 hour trading volume, over all recognised exchanges on www.coinmarketcap.com, surpassed US$100,000 on the 29th December.

On the 6th January, Carsen Klock said work was being carried out towards testing some code relating to masternodes. As of yet, it still looked like MN holders would receive 33% of the overall coin generation (average block rewards). This had not yet been finalised. Version 1.0.7.0 was still the current stable release.

Four days later, on the 10th January, exciting news was reported. Denarius cold storage cards had become publicly available for purchase at http://whopper.io/

"Whopper Wallet Cards are a secure way to store your coins for extended safe keeping, trading, or showing off to your friends, family, and co-workers. Whopper Wallet Cards are waterproof and more durable than paper wallets, and are printed on high quality PVC cards with an industry leading IDP 70 smart security printer.

Each card receives a randomly generated public and private address and is stored securely within the printer under triple lock and key and is securely destroyed after the roll is depleted. Whopper Crypto never stores any of your information and you are the sole owner of the public and private key. A security scratch off sticker conceals the private key QR code for easy unloading of your coins."

A decision had been made to skip version 1.0.8.0 in favour of moving immediately towards version 2.0.0.0. All code and feature updates would be carried forward. A testnet blockchain had launched to test the code, especially masternodes, ready for version 2.0.0.0. As many testers as possible were welcome to help. A new version of proof of stake was confirmed as working on testnet.

On the 29th January, an exchange called SouthXchange initiated four DNR related trading pairs (DNR against USD, BTC, LTC and BCH). It was the first exchange to introduce the DNR/USD trading pair. At the time of publication of this book, it is the second most popular exchange on which Denarius is trading.

On the 24th February, after a lengthy and demanding testing phase, version 2.0.0.0 was made available for users to download and install. It was vital for users to install it before block number 640,000 after which the calculated proof of stake reward structure would change from *CoinAge * 0.06 / 365 / COIN* to *CoinAge * 0.06 / 365*.

Also, a Masternode Tab and GUI were included in version 2.0.0.0 (see pages 58 and 59). From this time, it was possible to utilise a DNR Hybrid Masternode if and only if one was willing to secure it with 5,000 DNR collateral. Masternode holders would begin receiving 33% of total block rewards after block number 645,000.

On the 1st March 2018, Carsen Klock recommended DNR traders to use either CoinExchange or SouthXchange, because they had already updated to version 2.0.0.0. There were doubts whether or not Cryptopia had done so, or if they were having backlog issues. He reiterated the importance of updating, because old clients would not accept new timestamped blocks.

On the following day, it was reported that 37 Hybrid DNR Masternodes were online. A website was created later at https://denarius.host which shows statistics including those associated with DNR Hybrid Masternodes.

Another wallet client update was released on the 4th March. It basically opened up support for atomic swaps on the decentralised BarterDEX exchange created by Komodo. People questioned if it was a mandatory update. Carsen Klock said:

> "Nope, a future release will be more than likely, but this one is not, but of course, recommended, if you stay on oldcode/old clients you will be unsupported really. It would be ideal for everyone to update to v2.0.2 if they can. I understand I have had a lot of updates recently, so I may just make one big mandatory one here in the future, but you should be on minimum v2.0.0.0 for PoS/Masternode payment improvements which is mandatory, v2.0.2.0 isn't but for gettxout support etc. you want the latest."

A few hours later, on the 4th March, the first atomic swap occurred on the DNR Blockchain.

Two days later, a total of 13 atomic swaps had been executed. A description of atomic swaps was posted on the official Denarius Bitcointalk thread:

> "An atomic swap is a direct trade between two different coins running on two separate blockchains; there are no centralised-exchange websites or other third-parties required for this trade. The technology enables common users to bypass the labyrinth of website-exchanges currently necessary to purchase cryptocurrencies. Once implemented, the atomic swap will allow common users to trade ad purchase any desired coin directly within their own wallets.
>
> The first step in performing an atomic swap is you and other party needs to agree on an exchange rate and also have available UTXOs. For example, you can go from BTC ->LTC, LTC->DNR, DNR->BTC and any other combination of currencies. Atomic swaps can be performed with a wide range of cryptocurrencies with Denarius, which will, one day, open up the doors for more fully decentralised exchanges and less reliance on 3rd parties."

On the 10th March, the community were notified that Denarius had been fully integrated with the decentralised exchange BarterDEX (soon to be rebranded). Secondly, it was also integrated into the KMD Agama Desktop Wallet. He described the Komodo Platform team as fantastic.

One day before the anticipated timestamp of block number 640,000, Cryptopia confirmed that they had updated to the most recent release. Members of the community were relieved to hear this news.

On the 16th March, the proof of stake fix (staking reward significantly increased) kicked in:

**Block #640,000 (Reward 3 DNR) March 16th 2018 at 09:12:47 PM UTC**

On the 17th March, another wallet update was released. Version 2.0.5.0 introduced further features to make Denarius more secure and reliable. The proof of stake fix was confirmed as working as expected.

Members of the community were joyous as they witnessed block number 645,000 timestamp on the 18th March. Approximately 160 DNR Hybrid Masternodes were now online as payments became active thereafter.

**Block #645,000 (Reward 0.00230136 DNR) March 18th 2018 at 08:24:47 AM UTC**

A thriving Denarius community continues to discuss, develop and devote time towards making the coin as competitive as possible. There are plans to implement further features as well as build on existing ones.

Recently, a new wallet client update was released. Version 2.5.0.0 introduced code optimisations to make syncing times faster. Other improvements can be read in the appendix on page 62. Users must update before block number 900,000, otherwise they will find themselves unable to connect to the blockchain.

# APPENDIX

# v1.0.0.0

 carsenk released this on 14 Jun 2017 · 323 commits to master since this release

## Assets

| | |
|---|---|
| 🗇 Denarius-OSX-v1000.dmg | 23 MB |
| 🗇 Denarius-QT.zip | 17 MB |
| 🗋 Source code (zip) | |
| 🗋 Source code (tar.gz) | |

First Release of Denarius! Launched 6/14/2017

v1.0.0.0 Windows QT Binary available below (Updated 6/21/2017)
v1.0.0.0 macOS QT .dmg available below (Updated 6/18/2017)

# Denarius v1.0.1.0

carsenk released this on 5 Jul 2017 · 280 commits to master since this release

## Assets

| | |
|---|---|
| 🗇 Denarius-QT.zip | 11.4 MB |
| 🗋 Source code (zip) | |
| 🗋 Source code (tar.gz) | |

7-5-2017 - Small updates to checkpoints, kernel and keys.

This update is not mandatory.

# v1.0.2.0

carsenk released this on 10 Jul 2017 · 280 commits to master since this release

## Assets

📁 Denarius-QT.zip        11.8 MB

🗎 Source code (zip)

🗎 Source code (tar.gz)

**Denarius v1.0.2.0 is now available!**

-Added Market Tab
-Market Information for DNR/BTC, DNR/USD, BTC/USD, and DNR Market Cap
-Statistic Tab contains Market Cap now
-Under the hood stuff for the next update
-DNR to BTC or USD calculator

# v1.0.3.0

carsenk released this on 17 Jul 2017 · 259 commits to master since this release

## Assets

📁 blockchain072017.zip        53.5 MB

📁 Denarius-QT.zip        11.8 MB

📁 Denarius-v1030.dmg        36.9 MB

🗎 Source code (zip)

🗎 Source code (tar.gz)

Denarius v1.0.3.0

-Updated Market Info Tab
-Under the hood changes for next release
-Updated About dialog
-Added another checkpoint

# v1.0.4.0

 carsenk released this on 31 Jul 2017 · 248 commits to master since this release

## Assets

| | |
|---|---|
| 📋 Denarius-QT.zip | 11.1 MB |
| 📋 Denarius-v1040.dmg | 17.7 MB |
| 🗂 Source code (zip) | |
| 🗂 Source code (tar.gz) | |

Denarius v1.0.4.0 is now available!

-Added calculated USD Balance on Overview page
-Removed old Tor integration code and libevent dep requirement
-Added addnode RPC command (You can now do in console window or with <./denariusd addnode ipaddress>)
-Cleaned up makefiles
-Fixed some staking verbiage in QT wallet
-Fixed UPNP on Compiled Windows QT (Should now sync easier for most)
-Added another checkpoint

# v1.0.5.0

carsenk released this on 19 Aug 2017 · 238 commits to master since this release

## Assets

| | |
|---|---|
| 📋 Denarius-QT.zip | 11.1 MB |
| 📋 DenariusInstaller.exe | 11.9 MB |
| 📋 Denarius-v1050.dmg | 18.8 MB |
| 🗂 Source code (zip) | |
| 🗂 Source code (tar.gz) | |

Denarius v1.0.5.0

-Added BTC Total to Overview in Wallet QT (Calculates your current DNR * Current BTC Price per DNR)
-Fixed Checkboxes, Checkboxes are now visible throughout the wallet
-Added more checkpoints
-Fixed Coin Control Dialog Styling
-Fixed a small bug with units
-Added DNR Trade Link to Overview
-Released Windows Installer for Denarius-QT

# v1.0.6.0

carsenk released this on 5 Sep 2017 · 226 commits to master since this release

## Assets

| | |
|---|---|
| 🗒 Denarius-QT.zip | 11.2 MB |
| 🗒 DenariusInstaller.exe | 12 MB |
| 🗒 bootstrap.dat | 139 MB |
| 🗒 Denarius-v1060.dmg | 16.7 MB |
| 🗋 Source code (zip) | |
| 🗋 Source code (tar.gz) | |

# Denarius v1.0.6.0

- Moved Backup Wallet from "File" to "Settings"
- **Added a new intro dialog** upon first launch or detection of no datadir, it allows you to easily select a datadir location for Denarius
  (Your datadir will contain the Denarius blockchain, your wallet data, peer data, and is also where you will create or add your denarius.conf if needed)
- Added **dumpbootstrap** RPC command, (Usage: dumpbootstrap [destination] [blocknumber])
- Added **gethashespersec** RPC command, (Usage: gethashespersec, It will return the current network GH/sec rate)
- Added **createmultisig** RPC command, (Usage: createmultisig [nsignature] [mkey, mkey], It will return a JSON object with the address and redeemScript)
- **Added Multisig** option under "File" in the QT, Create Multisig Addresses or Send Funds!
- **Added new txdb-bdb (Berkley DB)**, this is untested and still recommended to use "USE_LEVELDB=1" when building the QT
- **Added a Staking Tab** in the wallet with staking estimation information *(This is still in its very early stages and provides estimates)*
- Added another checkpoint

# v1.0.7.0

carsenk released this on 7 Oct 2017 · 218 commits to master since this release

## Assets

| | |
|---|---|
| bootstrap277757-10-6-2017.zip | 136 MB |
| Denarius-QT.zip | 11.3 MB |
| DenariusInstaller.exe | 12 MB |
| Denarius-v1070.dmg | 22.9 MB |
| bootstrap340k-11-03-2017.zip | 164 MB |
| bootstrap415000-12-2-2017.zip | 198 MB |
| Source code (zip) | |
| Source code (tar.gz) | |

## Denarius v1.0.7.0

10/8/2017 - v1.0.7.0 - Miscellaneous Fixes
-Added new bootstrap.dat (Block 277757, 10/6/2017, Compressed .zip)

c60c1bc - Updated getblock RPC Command, Inline with newer Bitcoin Core Releases.
c85ae7a - v1.0.7.0 Increment and Checkpoints
7503976 - Removed Staking Estimation Reward Temporarily
4662285 - Fixed Display of Market Values
61a0e84 - Fixed Overview Page USD Balance Display
a35d228 - Renamings for Deb Building
3e55d40 - More Staking Estimation Tab changes & Checkpoints
da22e61 - Updated Overview Page GUI
8a91064 - Updated TX Icons
3e666fe - More icons and GUI Fix
f15fe5b - More GUI Fixes
1380458 - Updated Makefiles

Side note: A new branch labelled "DNS" was created which will be for potentially a future v1.5, this branch will include code for Namecoin names functionality and a DNS Server that will interface with it. It is still in its very early stages and needs feedback from developers and fixes. It is not recommended to run this branch on any production servers or important wallets.

Windows and macOS Binaries are available below, along with the blockchain bootstrap up until block 277757.

## v1.0.8.0

carsenk released this on 19 Dec 2017 · 2 commits to addrindex since this release

### Assets

📁 bootstrap-450k-12-19-17.zip                                                    215 MB

⬇ Source code (zip)

⬇ Source code (tar.gz)

# Denarius v1.0.8.0

New Denarius RPC Commands:

- Added searchrawtransactions rpc command
- Added getrichlist rpc command
- Added updaterichlist rpc command
- Added resetrichlist rpc command
- Added getblock_old rpc command (Old version of the getblock command prior to Denarius v1.0.7.0, Bitcoin Core v0.10 and earlier style)

Under the hood changes:

- Added Rich List GUI to the Denarius QT Wallet
- Corrected the .pro file to USE_LEVELDB by default

Maybes:

- Refactoring COutPoint/CInPoint/CTxIn/CTxOut into core.h Potentially*
- Refactoring CTxMempool into txmempool.h/.cpp, Function changes Potentially*

Added the new flag "-reindexaddr" to index the new address DB, this must be indexed to run the richlist commands or use the Rich List GUI, reindexing the address DB can take awhile 15+ minutes, especially if it is your first time running -reindexaddr, also running updaterichlist or resetrichlist will take awhile to get the data.

*WIP - It is not recommended to run anything in this v1.0.8.0 branch until production release on your main wallet, use a VM or test machine/wallet.

12/19/2017 - Pre-Release Notes, No Binaries/Release available yet, compile from branch 'addrindex'.

-Added bootstrap Block 450k 12-19-2017 (v1.0.7.0)

# Denarius v2.0.0.0

carsenk released this on 24 Feb · 34 commits to master since this release

### Assets

| | |
|---|---|
| bootstrap-584k.zip | 266 MB |
| Denarius-v2-Win-32bit.zip | 11.8 MB |
| Denarius-32bit.exe | 25.3 MB |
| DenariusInstaller-32bit.exe | 12.5 MB |
| Denarius-v2-Win-64bit.zip | 11.6 MB |
| Denarius-64bit.exe | 24.3 MB |
| Denarius-2.0.0.0.dmg | 21.1 MB |
| chaindata-2-27-18.zip | 626 MB |
| Source code (zip) | |
| Source code (tar.gz) | |

# Denarius v2.0.0.0 (MANDATORY UPDATE)

New Denarius Hybrid Masternodes and PoS Fix!

You must update before block 640,000!

New Denarius RPC Commands:

- Added searchrawtransactions rpc command
- Added getrichlist rpc command
- Added updaterichlist rpc command
- Added resetrichlist rpc command
- Added getblock_old rpc command (Old version of the getblock command prior v1.0.7.0)
- Added masternode rpc commands
- Added darksend rpc command
- Added spork rpc command
- Added getpoolinfo rpc command
- Added denominate rpc command
- Updated getblocktemplate rpc command (Contains masternode payment/payee information for pools)

Under the hood changes:

- Added Rich List GUI to the Denarius QT Wallet
- Corrected the .pro file to USE_LEVELDB by default
- Refactored COutPoint/CInPoint/CTxIn/CTxOut into core.h
- Refactored CTxMempool into txmempool.h/.cpp
- Fixed Market Cap and Bitcoin Price Formatting in Market Tab
- Added Refresh Button to Overview of all balances, easily refresh USD/BTC Estimated Totals
- Added DarkSend GUI to Denarius QT Wallet (WIP)
- Added DarkSend, InstantX, and Spork structuring code to Denarius
- Added Masternode Tab & GUI to Denarius QT Wallet
- Added Masternodes to Denarius blockchain, live on: ~March 14th 2018 (**Block 645,000**)
- Masternodes will require 5,000 DNR to utilize and will be provided 33% of the block reward
- Fixed Proof of Stake Rewards from CoinAge * 0.06 / 365 / COIN to CoinAge * 0.06 / 365 (Goes live on **Block 640,000**)
- Removed IRC Node Connection Code (This should help with anti-virus false positives for Denarius, but heuristics may still complain)
- Fixed denariusd compilation with different boost versions on other Linux flavors
- Fixed darksend, multisig, and other non-string rpc command conversions
- Added Darksend Rounds to Coin Control in QT and Denominate button
- Added Tools menu in Denarius QT, easily access your denarius.conf or masternode.conf
- Added the new flag "-reindexaddr" to index the new address DB, this must be indexed to run the richlist commands or use the Rich List GUI, reindexing the address DB can take awhile 15+ minutes, especially if it is your first time running -reindexaddr, also running updaterichlist or resetrichlist will take awhile to get the data.
- Added Terms of Use for utilizing Denarius
- Added Proof of Data to Denarius, Image timestamping on the blockchain for proof of ownership
- Updated denariusd to warn less during compile
- Added Proof of Burn to masternode payments if masternodes are not found upon boot
- Updated QT to display Mined/Staked coins properly
- Added a ton more of updates and fixes and additions! (So many commits 174 roughly...lol)

# v2.0.0.1

 carsenk released this on 3 Mar · 1 commit to trade since this release

## Assets

| | |
|---|---|
| 🗂 Denarius-v2.0.0.1-Win64.zip | 12.8 MB |
| 🗋 Source code (zip) | |
| 🗋 Source code (tar.gz) | |

Denarius v2.0.0.1

This releases notes are coming soon. This release is still a work in progress.

-Cryptopia.co.nz Trading Tab Added, Works with your private API keys from Cryptopia.co.nz
-API Keys can be saved, when saved, they are encrypted with standard AES encryption.
-Seed Nodes Updated to latest known seeds
-Added new checkpoints
-Updated QT to QT5
-Fixed My Masternode Tab "Create..." button, actually creates masternode.conf now.

# v2.0.2.0

carsenk released this on 4 Mar · 9 commits to master since this release

## Assets

| | |
|---|---|
| 🗂 Denarius-v2.0.2-Win64.zip | 12.8 MB |
| 🗂 Denarius-2.0.2.0.dmg | 18.4 MB |
| 🗂 chaindata.zip | 992 MB |
| 🗋 Source code (zip) | |
| 🗋 Source code (tar.gz) | |

Denarius v2.0.2.0

Join our Discord chat! https://discord.gg/mDTM3JN

-Added gettxout rpc command for BarterDEX support
-Added importaddress rpc command and Watch Only addresses.
(Using importaddress is similar to importprivkey and can cause your client to lag since it causes the wallet to run a -rescan)
-Fixed some random things
-Implemented BIP65 CHECKLOCKTIMEVERIFY support
-Cleaned up some code

Get BarterDEX with DNR Atomic Swap Native & Electrum SPV Support here until official release:
https://github.com/carsenk/BarterDEX/releases/tag/0.8.9-rc

# Denarius v2.0.5.0

carsenk released this on 19 Mar · 2 commits to master since this release

## Assets

| | |
|---|---|
| 📁 Denarius-v2.0.5.0-Win64.zip | 12.8 MB |
| 📁 Denarius-2.0.5.0.dmg | 17.3 MB |
| 📄 Source code (zip) | |
| 📄 Source code (tar.gz) | |

# Denarius v2.0.5.0

- Added Litemode!
- (Add the litemode=1 flag to your denarius.conf to run your wallet in "Litemode", running your wallet in litemode prevents your node from processing masternode/darksend/instantx messages.)
- Running your node in litemode will help with current performance issues with denariusd and the Denarius-QT
- Running your node in litemode will NOT allow the use of masternode information/services, you cannot run a masternode in litemode!
- Added 'litemode' flag return to the getinfo rpc command
- Added Litemode On/Off in the Information Tab in the QT
- Added checkpoints
- Added kernel modifier checkpoints
- Added checks to listunspent rpc command for spent coins (atomic swaps)
- Added 'masternode' flag information to getinfo rpc command
- PoS Reward Fix is confirmed working!
- Started work on UTXO index

# Denarius v2.5.0.0

 carsenk released this 18 hours ago

## Assets

| | |
|---|---|
| 📄 Denarius-v2.5-Win64.zip | 12.7 MB |
| 📄 Denarius-2.5.0.0.dmg | 17.6 MB |
| 📄 denariusd-2.5.0.0_centos7.tar.gz | 2.75 MB |
| 📄 denariusd-2.5.0.0_ubuntu16.tar.gz | 3.63 MB |
| 📄 Source code (zip) | |
| 📄 Source code (tar.gz) | |

# Mandatory Update Denarius v2.5!

-Protocol Update (25213 now)
-Removed Litemode
-Removed Trading API (May add back in, in a future update)
-Reworked threading for Masternodes
-Removed Darksend

(We want to bring a better privacy method of sending coins in Denarius, hence the removal of Darksend, we are currently looking into potentially integrating libzerocoin in a future release.)
-Removed Instantx
-Optimized Keypool
-General Optimization and Fixes
-Forced port 9999 for mainnet masternodes and 19999 for testnet
-Updated Watch Only Addresses/Support
-Optimized Syncing Speeds (Improved to around 200-400 blocks per second vs. old 3 blocks per second)
-Optimized Wallet
-Fixed sending transactions with a narration
-Added Watch Only balances in QT if any watch only addresses are available
-Added the ignoring of staking inputs for exact amounts of 5,000 DNR for masternodes
-Updated the listtransactions RPC command to provide vout information
-Old Nodes will no longer connect to our current protocol of 25213 after block 900,000, so ensure that you are updated to v2.5 on all of your Denarius and denariusd nodes before block 900,000.

If you have a node running do the following to update it:

```
./denariusd stop && cd .. && git pull && cd src && make clean && make -f makefile.unix
```